Artistic Affirmations

Artistic Affirmations

G.A. Schelin

Soothe your soul and quieten your mind - daily affirmations and coloring: Where self-care becomes your masterpiece...

Dedication

Dedicated to the seekers of serenity, and the dreamers of vibrant possibilities. May the strokes of your imagination find solace within these pages, pouring the canvas of your soul with joy, mindfulness, and a kaleidoscope of emotions. This book is dedicated to the beautiful journey of self-discovery, where every hue tells a tale and each moment of coloring becomes a brushstroke in the masterpiece of your own existence. Embrace the therapeutic magic within, and may your world be forever painted with peace and inspiration.

First printing, 2024.
ISBN: 978-0-7961-5565-8 (print)

Firefox Publishing
11A Harvey Road, Harfield Village.
Cape Town, Western Cape,
South Africa, 7708

@firefoxpublishing

"May you be the reason someone smiles today"
Anonymous

"Every accomplishment starts with the decision to try"
John F. Kennedy

"Be the change you want to see in the world"
Mahatma Ghandi

"Believe that you can and you're halfway there"
Theodore Roosevelt

"A person who never made a mistake, never tried something new" – Albert Einstein

"The journey of a thousand miles begins with one step" - Lao Tzu

"I have not failed. I have just found 10 000 ways that won't work" - Thomas Edison

"It's all about finding the calm in the chaos"
Donna Karan

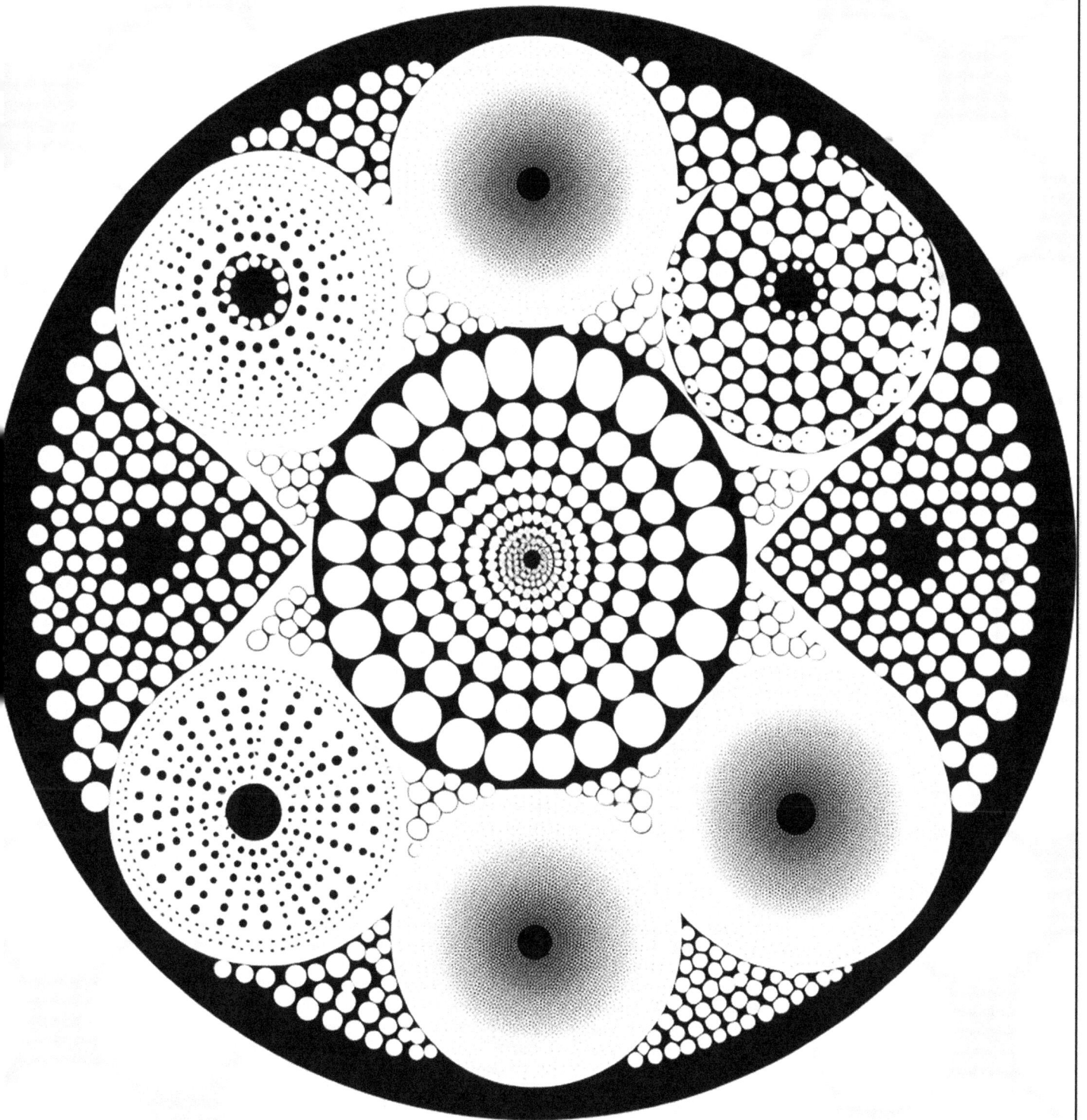

"The best way out, is always through" – Robert Frost

"If it's still in your mind, then it's worth taking the risk"
Paulo Coehlo

"Change is inevitable. Growth is optional"
John C. Maxwell

"Without pressure. There would be no diamonds."
Thomas Carlyle

"Life always offers you a second chance

and it's called, tomorrow" - Stephen King

"Don't call it a dream.
Call it a plan"
Anonymous

"Quality is the presence of value, not the absence of mistakes"
Anonymous

"Failure is not the opposite of success, it is a part of success"
Arianna Huffington

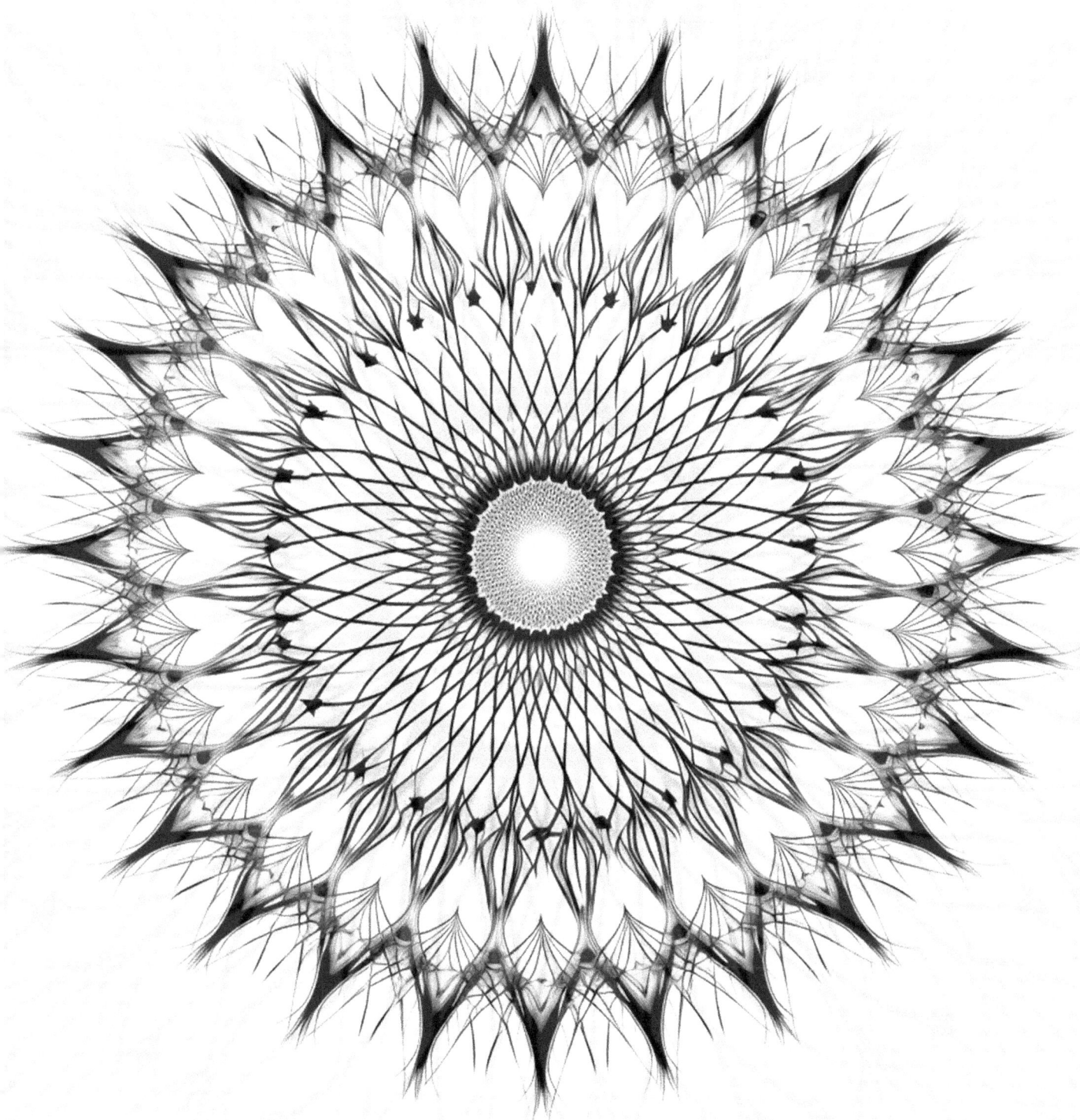

"Don't start something to test the waters. Start something to make the waves" - Anonymous

"Never argue with a fool, people may not know the difference"
Mark Twain

"The world is changed by your example, not by your opinion"
Paulo Coehlo

"Never measure your success, by someone else's ruler"
Anonymous

"Starve your distractions. Feed your focus"
Steve Weatherford

"Set peace of mind as your highest goal, and
organise your life around it"
Brian Tracy

"*Today I choose calm over chaos, serenity over stress, peace over perfection, grace over grit, faith over fear*"
Mary Davis

"Talk to yourself, like someone you love"
Brene Brown

"Words satisfy your mind, but silence satifies your soul."
Nitin Namdeo

"Sometimes what looks like an obstacle in your path,
is actually a gift moving you in a different direction"
Jane Lee Logan

"Confidence is not they will like me. Confidence is
I'm fine if they don't" - Anonymous

"Don't let yesterday, take too much
up of today" - Will Rogers

"Embrace uncertainty. Some of the most beautiful chapters
in our lives won't have a title until much later"
Anonymous

"You want to be the pebble in the pool
that creates the ripples for change" - Tim Cook

"You are what you believe yourself to be"
Paulo Coehlo

"The people who are crazy enough to think they can change the world, are the ones who do"
Steve Jobs

"It always seems impossible, until it's done"
Nelson Mandela

"*Figure out who you are, and then do it on purpose*"
Dolly Parton

"Don't let the darkness of the past, cover the brightness of the future" - Anonymous

In each stroke a whispered tale untold,
Grateful hearts embrace the beauty they unfold.

GS Schelin

www.ingramcontent.com/pod-product-compliance
Lightning Source LLC
Chambersburg PA
CBHW081721270326
41933CB00017B/3246

9 780796 155658